TWELVE PIANO-FORTE SONATAS OF
L. GIUSTINI DI PISTOJA

First published in 1732, and now edited in facsimile by

ROSAMOND E. M. HARDING
Ph.D., Cantab.

CAMBRIDGE: AT THE UNIVERSITY PRESS

1933

To 'I. M.'

PREFACE

THE Sonatas reprinted in the present volume are probably the earliest music for the pianoforte[1] of which an exact date is known. They are dedicated to the Infante Don Antonio of Portugal[2] by D. Giovanni de Seixas[3] who, in his dedication, reminds the Prince that he had heard them with pleasure during his—de Seixas'—visit to Italy and that musicians of sound judgment declared the music to be in "excellent taste".

Of the composer Lodovico Giustini nothing is known except that he published a

[1] First recognised by Alfred James Hipkins as being the earliest pianoforte music and referred to as such in his *History of the Pianoforte*, Novello Primer No. 52, London, 1896, Part 3, p. 99. Since referred to as probably the earliest dated music for the pianoforte by Fausto Torrefranca in *Le Origini Italiane del Romanticismo Musicale*, Torino, 1930, pp. 366, 370.

It will be remembered that Sebastian Bach wrote nothing for the pianoforte and Carl Philipp Emanuel Bach thought the pianoforte only fit for Rondos and wrote little of importance for it; Mozart's first important works for this instrument began in 1763; and Johann Christian Bach and Muzio Clementi, the two composers who did most to popularise the pianoforte, wrote their first works for it as late as 1768 and 1773 respectively.

[2] Younger son of King Pedro II. Born 1645; died 1757.

[3] Possibly related to José Antonio Carlos de Seixas (b. 1704; d. 1742), organist of the Church of St Basil, Lisbon; a gifted composer of vocal and instrumental music.

volume of XII Clavier Sonatas at Amsterdam in 1736[1] and that he was an "instrumental composer".[2]

The Sonatas appear, at first sight, to differ little from those written for the ordinary harpsichord. The differences in sound indicated in the score by the terms *forte, piano* or the series of terms *forte, piano, più piano*[3] and even *più forte*[4] could be produced by registration upon a large harpsichord. But, as often occurs in music, the directions contained in the score do not fully represent the intention of the composer.

Giustini lived at Pistoja, near Florence; and Florence had been the seat of the discussions concerning the revival of classical drama on the lines adopted by the ancient Greek tragedians which resulted in the invention of the Cantata, a secular song for solo voice set in declamatory recitative.

Attention was drawn to the fact that the emotional effect of a musical phrase could be intensified as could that of a line of poetry by an appropriate use of inflections of sound.

The harpsichord and the organ were incapable of these delicate inflections. Dissatisfaction with these instruments spread to other countries. Hans Haydn of Nuremberg

[1] No copy of this work appears to exist.
[2] Gerber, *Neues historischbiographisches Lexikon der Tonkünstler*, Leipzig, 1812–14.
[3] Giustini does not begin to use this series of terms until Sonata No. 6.
[4] One instance only: p. 35 (Sonata No. 6; Dolce).

attempted in 1600 to make the harpsichord capable of the "inflections of voices" by means of a ringbow mechanism; for he did not consider the changes obtained by the use of stops were satisfactory as the tone always remained at the same unbroken level.[1]

[1] "Es haben die *Componisten* sonderlich ein zeithero mit allem Fleiss dahin getrachtet, wie sie die *Musicam* im Gesang aufs höchst bringen möchten, also, dass sie nunmehr nicht wol höher zu steigen hat. Die *Musicalische Instrumenta* aber betreffend, obwol an etlichen grosse Mängel gefunden, als dass sie der schönsten Zier, nämlich der *Moderation* der Stimmen mangeln, so hat sich doch bei so viel kunstreichen *Instrumentisten,* so jederzeit gewesen, keiner unterstanden, demselben Gebrechen abzuhelfen und die *Moderation* der Stimmen auch ins *Clavir* zu bringen.

"Wieviel aber daran gelegen, die Stimme zu *formiren,* das wissen diejenigen, so in den *Capellen,* die jungen Knaben und *Cantores* abzurichten pflegen. Es verstehts auch zwar sonsten fast ein jeder, was es für ein Uebelstand nur an einem gemeinen *Oratore* ist, wann derselb im aus sprechen mit Erhebung und Niederlassung der . . . [69] Stimme, wie es der Text und *affectus* erfordern, keinen *docorum* [sic] hält, sondern immer in gleichen Ton an einander unabgesetzt fortredet. So nun dasselbige im Reden, vielmehr ist es im Singen verdriesslich zu hören.

"Es ist aber ein jedes *Clavirtes Instrument,* sowol die Orgeln, welche doch sonsten, was die *gravitatem* belangt, den Vorzug vor allen andern *Instrumenten* haben, als auch alle andere Pfeiffwerk mit diesem Mangel behaft, dass sie nicht *moderirt,* noch die Stimmen zum lauten oder stillen Klang und *Sono* gezwungen werden können, sondern es gibt und behält die Pfeiffe ihren Laut in gleichem Ton, wie auch der *Instrumentist* den *Clavem* angreift, und ist unmüglich [sic] die Stimme zu stärken oder zu lindern; welches aber einer mit dem Bogen auf der Geigen, nach dem er stark oder leise drauf streicht und aufdrückt, thun kann. Und ist also der *Instrumentist* auf dem *Clavir* gefangen, dass er seine *affecten* nicht, wie sonsten auf der Geigen (ob er schon den Text darauf auch nicht aussprechen kann) dennoch kann zu merken geben, ob traurige, fröliche, ernstliche oder schimpfliche Gedanken in ihme sein: Welches aber allein durch die

Vincenzo Galilei[1] stated that such a *Geigenwerk* had been considered before. A few years after Galilei's death another attempt was made, for we read of instruments called *Piano e forte* in letters addressed to Alfonso II, Duke of Modena, by Paliarino in 1598.[2] But these experiments were unsatisfactory and in Italy, at least, all hope of making the harpsichord capable of the "inflections of voices" seems soon to have been abandoned, and the experiments in relation to dynamic expression had to be confined to voices and strings and such wind instruments as were capable of reproducing them.

About 1709, however, the problem of making the harpsichord capable of inflections was solved by Bartolommeo Cristofori of Padua (but at this time living at Florence) by substituting hammers in place of the jacks. He called the new harpsichord the *Gravicembalo col piano e forte*.

Moderation der Stimme geschehen muss. Und ob man wol in den Orgeln mit Ab- und Zuziehung der Register, jetzt ein stilles, sanftes, liebliches, bald wiederumb ein lautes Getön und Geschrei machen kann, so heisst doch dasselbige, weil es in gleichem Ton still oder laut bleibt, keine *Moderation*, sondern es ist ein ungeformirte, ungebrochene Stimm, wie hier vorn von einer unabgesetzten Rede gesagt worden." [Hans Haydn, quoted by Michael Praetorius in *Syntagma*, II. Teil, *Von den Instrumenten*. Reprint: Breitkopf und Härtel, Leipzig, 1894 (XLIV, Cap. S. 80, 81).]

[1] Born in Florence about 1533 and died there in 1591, had taken a leading part in the discussions at Florence already referred to on page vi. Father of the Astronomer Galileo Galilei.

[2] Grove's *Dictionary of Music and Musicians*, Art. *Pianoforte*, 3rd ed., London, 1928, vol. IV, p. 150.

Surprise that anyone should succeed in making the harpsichord capable of these inflections is clearly stated by the Marchese Scipione Maffei, who discovered Cristofori and wrote a paper on the newly invented "harpsichord with the piano and forte". Experiments in dynamic expression consisting of contrasts of *piano* and *forte* and gradations from *forte* to *piano* were being tried with success at the great concerts at Rome.[1] Maffei says that no one would have thought it possible that these effects could be produced upon the harpsichord, but Cristofori had made three harpsichords upon which not only were the *forte* and *piano* possible but also *gradations* and shades of tone as on a violoncello.[2]

[1] Doubtless the Grand Accademie held at Cardinal Ottoboni's Palace every Monday evening under the direction of Arcangelo Corelli. The band would be composed almost entirely of bowed stringed instruments. See Burney, *A General History of Music*, London, 1789, vol. III, pp. 551, 552.

[2] "Egli è noto a chiunque gode della musica, che uno de' principali fonti, da' quali traggano i periti di quest' arte il segreto di singolarmente dilettar chi ascolta, è il piano, e'l fortezzo, sia nelle proposte e risposte, o sia quando con artifiziosa degradazione lasciandosi a poco a poco mancar la voce, si ripiglia poi ad un tratto strepitosamente: il quale artifizio è usato frequentemente, ed a meraviglia ne' gran concerti di Roma. . . . Ora di questa diversità ed alterazione di voce, nella quale eccellenti sono, fra gli altri, gli strumenti da arco, affatto privo è il gravecembalo; e sarebbe, da chi che sia, stata riputata una vanissima immaginazione il proporre di fabbricarlo in modo, che avesse questa dote. Con tutto cio, una sì ardita invenzione è stata non meno felicemente pensata, che eseguita in Firenze dal Sig. Bartolommeo Cristofali [sic], Padavano, Cembalista stipendiato dal Serenissimo Principe di Toscana. Egli ne ha finora

The influence of the Italian school of violin playing is clearly reflected in the harpsichord music of the period. Upon the newly invented pianoforte it now became possible not only to imitate the general style of violin music but to reproduce much of the dynamic pattern.

The effects of *forte* contrasted with *piano* and *gradations* of sound from *forte* to *piano* referred to by Maffei are found in Giustini's music. The series of terms *forte, piano, più piano* indicate a *gradual decrease* of tone. The music should be played expressively and in order to bring out its true significance the performer should imagine that he is conducting a choir of voices or a band of bowed stringed instruments.

Apart from the effects of dynamic expression the Sonatas do not present any striking features of construction. They are *Sonate da Camera* and differ little from others of this period.

Sonatas Nos. 1, 2, 5, 11 and 12 are in five movements, whilst the remaining seven are in four movements. The grouping of the individual movements is experimental.

fatti tre della grandezza ordinaria degli altri gravecembali, e son tutti riusciti perfettamente. Il cavare da questi maggiore o minore suono dipende dalla diversa forza, con cui dal vengono premuti i tasti, regolando la quale, si viene a sentire non soli il piano, e il forte, ma la degradazione, e diversità della voce, qual sarebbe in un violoncello." [Rimbault, *The Pianoforte*, London, 1860, pp. 95, 96, quoting Scipione Maffei: "Nuova Invenzione d' un Gravecembalo col piano, e forte, aggiunte alcune considerazioni sopra gl' istrumenti musicali". Art. in *Giornale dei Letterati d' Italia*, Tom. v, p. 144. Venezia, 1711.]

Two Gigas are placed together in Sonata No. 2, in C minor; the first is in the relative major and 3 : 8 tempo and marked *grave*; the second, in the tonic and 12 : 8 tempo, is marked *presto*. The tenth Sonata, in four movements, has Alemandas for the first and third movements in the same tempo and key. Three Sonatas (Nos. 1, 2 and 12) have as their terminal movement a Minuet. There are three examples of the Rondo; these occur in Sonatas Nos. 8, 9 and 11 (pp. 47, 54 and 64).

Giustini cannot be said to have a particular style. He was perhaps somewhat at a loss to know how to write for the new *Gravicembalo*. He has, in fact, tried various styles. The influence of the comic opera is the most apparent in the highly ornamented themes with their characteristic grace notes. In other Sonatas these ornaments disappear and the composer seems to be influenced by Leo's church music; this is particularly the case in the Canzone of the tenth Sonata (p. 58).

An example of an entirely different treatment is found in the *Affettuoso* of Sonata No. 5, the *Corrente* of Sonata No. 7 and the *Sarabanda* of Sonata No. 9; in these movements the composer is evidently thinking of the *Concerto Grosso* and he imitates the string tremolando in the *Corrente* of the seventh Sonata (p. 41).

There are three examples of the *Siciliana*, and another pastoral theme occurs in the *Andante* of the third Sonata where a shepherd's pipe tune in the right hand is supported in the left for a few bars by a droning bass in imitation of the bagpipes (pp. 14, 15).

The composer sometimes uses an experimental cadence in which the tonic and the dominant are sounded together in the last chord but one of the cadence, and makes a feature of this in the first movement of Sonata No. 5.[1]

Giustini's Pianoforte

The compass of the music is four octaves and one note B_1 to c''' and the composer has used all the chromatic notes within this limit as illustrated below:

[1] Position of experimental cadences. Sonata No. 1, *Balletto*, p. 1, l. 3; Sonata No. 1, *Sarabanda*, p. 3, l. 3; Sonata No. 3, *Andante*, p. 15, l. 1 and l. 3; Sonata No. 4, *Preludio*, p. 17, l. 3, and p. 18, l. 2; Sonata No. 5, *Preludio*, p. 23, l. 1 and l. 2, and p. 24, l. 1 and l. 2, Sonata No. 7, *Alemanda*, p. 39, l. 3; Sonata No. 7, *Corrente*, p. 41, l. 5 (tonic + dominant + mediant of the tonic); Sonata No. 11, *Dolce*, p. 62, l. 2.

It is probable that B_I to c''' was the compass of his keyboard. B is an unusual note as the terminal of a keyboard; when it occurs it is usually tuned to G. The compass of this instrument as it left the maker—Cristofori or one of his pupils—was probably G_I (apparently B_I) C–c'''. But Giustini must have tuned his pianoforte in equal temperament to admit of the music being played and in doing so he has given the B_I its true pitch.

Although the strings of Cristofori's pianofortes were slightly thicker than those he used for ordinary harpsichords, yet they were very thin, and this fact accounts for Giustini writing closely packed chords low down in the bass.

R. E. M. H.

Three copies of Giustini's pianoforte Sonatas of 1732 are known to exist. They are disposed as follows: (1) British Museum (perfect copy); (2) Mr Harold Reeves,[1] London (perfect copy); (3) Rowe Music Library, King's College, Cambridge (imperfect copy, wanting folios 57–64).

Giustini's pianoforte Sonatas are described in the British Museum Catalogue thus: "Giustini (Lodovico) Sonate da Cimbalo di piano, e forte detto volgarmente di martelletti....Opera prima. *Firenze, 1732, obl. fol. Engraved throughout*".

To this description may be added the following particulars: 38 leaves, 22·4 cm. × 31·9 cm. No water-mark. Plate mark, 19·6–20·2 cm. × 28·6 cm. Title and dedication, 2 leaves unnumbered. Music, 36 leaves, engraved on both sides except the last, engraved on one side only: in all 71 numbered pages, the last unnumbered and blank.

The engraving appears to be the work of two craftsmen. The hand of the second engraver appears on pp. 51, 54, 55 and 59.

A sign for a double sharp ✕ occurs on p. 47, l. 1, bars one and three of the right-hand part. The engravers use the following sign for a crotchet rest: ⸻, the other

[1] See Mr Harold Reeves' Catalogue No. 102, *Old Rare and Interesting Musical Works,* London, 1932, p. 14.

signs for rests are as usual. The music contains errors, and rests are omitted in various places. A select list of Errata is appended.

In conclusion I desire to express my thanks to the Trustees of the British Museum Library for permitting me to have the photographic copy of Giustini's Sonatas from which the present edition is taken, and to Messrs Breitkopf and Härtel of Leipzig for courteously permitting me to print the quotation on pp. vii–viii, footnote 1, from their edition of *Syntagma Musicum* by Praetorius.

Through the courtesy of the editor, I reprint the substance of an article entitled "The Earliest Pianoforte Music" which occurred in *Music and Letters*, Vol. XIII, No. 2, April, 1932.

I am obliged to various learned friends for helpful suggestions.

R. E. M. H.

ABBREVIATIONS

Acc. or *accs.*   = *acciaccatura* or *acciaccaturas.*

B. *or* Bs.   = bar *or* bars.

B.+   = last bar of the line.

Numerals in
roman figures = beat number in the bar.

L.   = line (i.e. pair of staves making
a line of music).

lt. = left hand.

rt. = right hand.

Note. The bars are numbered from left to right.
The first bar, whether *complete* or *incomplete*,
on each line is counted as No. 1.

Note. If the pitch of the last note in a bar is altered by an accidental this alteration holds for the first note of the following bar if it is on the same degree of the stave.

xvi

ERRATA

Page 2

L. 1, B. 2: there should be a bar line after the first group of four quavers.

L. 5, Bs. 8, 9, 10 rt.: F *sharp*, as in the two previous bars.

Page 3

L. 3, Bs. 5, 6 I rt.: read thus:

Page 4

L. 2, B.+ IV lt.: F *natural*.

Page 5

L. 2, B. 1 III lt.: E *natural*.

L. 4, B. 1 IV rt.: read second *acc.* as A *natural*.

Page 6

L. 1, B. 2 IV rt.: read second *acc.* as A *natural*.

L. 2, B. 3 IV rt.: read the *accs.* as D *natural* and E *natural*; the last quaver of the fourth beat should be E *flat*.

Page 6

L. 2, B. 3 IV lt.: read D *natural*.

L. 5, B. 12, last quaver, rt.: F *sharp*.

Page 7

L. 1, B.+ IV lt.: read F as a quaver.

L. 3, B. 5, last quaver, rt.: D *natural*.

Page 8

L. 4, B. 10 lt.: A *flat*.

L. 5, B. 8 II rt.: F *natural*.

Page 9

L. 1, Bs. 9, 10 I rt.: D *flat*.

Page 14

L. 3, B. 2 IV, first quaver, lt.: B *flat*.

Page 19

L. 2, B. 2 IV lt.: E (not F *sharp*).

xvii

Page 20

L. 3, B.+ I, second quaver, rt.: D *natural*.

L. 5, B. 1 I, second quaver, rt.: D *natural*.

Page 21

L. 2, B.+ lt.: D *sharp*.

Page 23

L. 2, B. 3 I rt.: read thus:

Page 24

L. 3, B. 4 I rt.: C *natural*.

L. 3, B. 5 I rt.: B *flat*.

Page 26

L. 5, B. 5 rt.: read thus:

Page 27

L. 3, B. 5 I rt.: C *natural*.

Page 28

L. 3, B. 4 I rt.: F *natural*.

Page 29

L. 3, B. 11, first quaver, lt.: D *sharp*.

L. 5, Bs. 4, 5, 6 rt.: read thus: (cf.
   L. 1, Bs. 7, 8 and 9).

Page 30

L. 1, B. 1 II rt.: read

L. 4, B.+ II, last quaver, rt.: F *natural*.

Page 31

L. 4, B. 1 rt.: read *acc.* as B *natural*.

Page 32

L. 3, B. 1 IV, last quaver, lt.: E *flat*.

Page 35

L. 4, B. 1 rt.: read *accs.* as B *natural* and C *sharp*.

Page 36

L. 2, B. 3 I, first semiquaver, lt.: F *sharp*.

L. 3, B. 2 rt.: read *acc.* as F *sharp*.

L. 3, B. 2 II rt.: read the upper *acc.* F *sharp* but the
   fourth semiquaver of the third beat as F *natural*.

Page 40

L. 4, B. 9 II, second semiquaver, rt.: F *natural*.

L. 5, B. 2 I rt.: C *sharp*.

L. 5, B. 8 I rt.: D *sharp*.

Page 41

L. 1, B. 3 lt.: A *sharp*.

L. 1, B. 5 rt.: D *sharp*.

L. 2, B. 4 I, third semiquaver, rt.: D *natural*.

Page 42

L. 1, B. 4 IV rt.: read thus:

L. 3, B. 7 read thus:

L. 4, B. 2 lt.: read G *sharp* dotted.

L. 5, Bs. 3, 7 VI rt.: A *natural*.

Page 43

L. 4, B. 1 I rt.: read thus: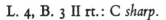

L. 4, B. 3 II rt.: C *sharp*.

Page 45

L. 2, B. 4 rt.: read thus:

Page 46

L. 3, B. 4 III, first quaver, lt.: E (not F *sharp*).

L. 3, B.+ I rt.: D *sharp*.

Page 47

L. 4, B. 8 I rt.: read *accs.* as F *sharp* and G *sharp* but the following G should be *natural*.

L. 5, B. 10 I rt.: F *sharp*.

L. 5, B. 11 rt.: F *sharp*.

Page 50

L. 2, B. 3 I rt.: read thus:

L. 3, B. 6 I rt.: read thus:

Page 51

L. 2, B. 4 I rt.: F *sharp*; but read F *natural* in the following bar.

Page 52

L. 1, B.+ II lt.: F *sharp* (cf. similar passage L. 2, B. 2).

L. 2, B. 4 IV, last quaver, lt.: read D (not F).

L. 3, Bs. 2, 4, 5 rt.: read *acc.* as C *sharp*. [N.B. B. 5 II, third semiquaver, rt.: read C *natural*.]

Page 55

L. 1, B.+ rt.: read thus:

Page 57

L. 4, B. 5 IV rt.: read thus:

L. 4, B.+ IV, last quaver, lt.: E *flat*.

Page 58

L. 2, B. 4 I rt.: D *flat*.

L. 4, B. 6 II rt.: D *flat*.

Page 59

L. 5, B.+ I rt.: E *natural*.

Page 60

L. 4, B. 11 I, upper note, lt.: D *flat*.

Page 62

L. 1, B. 2: there should be a bar line after the fourth crotchet (cf. L. 3, Bs. 4 and 5).

L. 3, B. 5 IV lt.: crotchet rest.

L. 3, B.+ II, second note in the chord, lt.: D *sharp*.

Page 63

L. 1, B. 2 I rt.: read thus:

L. 1, B. 8 I, second semiquaver, rt.: A *sharp*.

L. 3, B. 3 I rt.: read thus:

Page 65

L. 1, B. 2 lt.: read *acc.* as D *sharp* (not E).

L. 2, B.+ lt.: read the last crotchet E as a quaver.

L. 5 should be barred thus: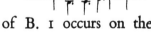

[N.B. the first half of B. 1 occurs on the previous line.]

Page 66

L. 1, B. 3 IX (i.e. III, third quaver) lt.: read G *sharp* (not E). Cf. L. 2, B. 1.

L. 2, B. 3 I rt.: G *natural*.

Page 67

L. 3, B. 2 V and VI rt.: C *sharp*.

L. 3, B. 3 rt.: read *acc.* as C *sharp*.

L. 3, B. 4 I, second note of the triplet, rt.: C *sharp*.

Page 69

L. 2, B.+ I rt.: read thus:

L. 3, B. 2 I rt.: read thus:

Page 69

L. 4, B. 2, last half, rt.: read thus:

L. 4, B. 6 rt.: read thus:

Page 70

L. 1, B.+ VI and XII lt.: C *sharp*.

Page 71

L. 1 and L 2, key signature, lt.: (i.e. Bass) F *sharp* (not G *sharp*).

L. 2, B. 2 VII, uppermost note of the chord, rt.: C *sharp* followed by C *natural* as indicated.

L. 4, B. 2 II, second semiquaver, lt.: C *natural*.

THE SONATAS

SONATE

Da Cimbalo di piano, e forte
detto volgarmente di martelletti

DEDICATE

A SUA ALTEZZA REALE

IL SERENISSIMO D. ANTONIO INFANTE

DI PORTOGALLO

E Composte

Da D. Lodovico Giustini di Pistoia

Opera prima

FIRENZE M DCCXXXII.

Altezza Reale

Presento col più deuoto rispetto a V.A.R. queste sonate, udite già da me con particolare soddisfazione nel mio soggiorno in Italia, e da quelli Intendenti di tal Professione giudicate di molto buon gusto. Io però non le pongo sotto i Reali suoi occhi, perchè le stimi adeguate al suo sopraffino discernimento, ma perchè nella loro artificiosa consonanza ci rappresentano in qualche modo quella celeste Armonia, che fanno nella bella, e ben ordinata Anima di V. A. R. le più rare Virtudi tra di loro in dolce lega congiunte. Spero che la R.A.V. la quale di questa soaue e diletteuole Saienza, come di tutte l'altre, sa dare così accertato giudizio non solamente, ma con somma marauiglia di chi ha l'onore di udirla, sa eziandio perfettamente esercitarla, non isdegnerà di compartire a questi Fogli un suo benignissimo sguardo in quelle ore, nelle quali suol dare à suoi sublimi pensieri qualche alleuiamento, e riposo. Supplico umilmente V. A. R. a continuare sopra di me la sua Sourana, e benefica Protezione, e a permettermi che io abbia la sospirata gloria di protestarmi con profondissimo ossequio

Di V. A. R.

Vmilissimo Seruo
D. Giovanni de Seixas.

SUONATA I

2

4

SUONATA II

8

Giga

Grave

forte

Minuet

12

SUONATA III

14

SUONATA IV.

20

Suonata V

24

Tempo di Gavotta

SUONATA. VI.

32

SUONATA VII

44

SUONATA VIIII

Allegro

50

SUONATA IX.

52

53

SUONATA X

Canzone Tempo di Gauotta

SUONATA XI

Segue

64

SUONATA XII